To Know Bedrock

For Graham.
With love,
Sharon

To Know Bedrock

Sharon Black

P_indrop Press

Published 2011 by
Pindrop Press
Mallards
Steers Place
Hadlow
Tonbridge
TN11 0HA

www.pindroppress.com

ISBN 978-0-9567822-3-6

A catalogue record for this book is available from the British Library.

Typeset by Pindrop Press.

Printed in Great Britain and the USA by Lightning Source.

Cover image: *Hebrides* by Isis Olivier; oil on paper, 110 x 90 cm, 2009

Acknowledgements

Versions of some of these poems have appeared in the following magazines: *Aesthetica, Agenda, Envoi, The Frogmore Papers, The Interpreter's House, Iota, The New Writer, Mslexia, Orbis;* and in the following anthologies: *Storm at Galesburg, The Visitors , Glimmer, Feeding the Cat, Kaleidoscope: an anthology of sequences, A Roof of Red Tiles* (all Cinnamon Press), *All the Way Home* (Leaf Books) and *Up to Our Necks in It* (Black Tulip Books). I gratefully acknowledge the support of these publications and their editors.

I would like to thank Bill Greenwell for his teaching and encouragement; Susan Richardson for her detailed reading of the manuscript and her help in pulling it all together; Lucy Wadham for her canny eye; Roselle Angwin for her island inspiration; Jan Fortune, Crysse Morrison and Esther Morgan for their many starting points; my fellow poets at Poetry Spiral and at Bill's online 'clinics'; and last, but definitely not least, my wonderful editor and publisher, Jo Hemmant.

For Alex, my bedrock

Contents

Insomniac

She writes when dreams won't come,
when the house is crouched in darkness
and her husband's eyes
are a folded prayer book.

Only the clock, slugging restless seconds
round on the wheel of its back
with the strength of Sisyphus,
rucks the silence.

The moon is a net
in the sea of the night,
shoals flicker and dart
beyond its yawning mouth.

She traces her fingers across the weeping pane,
traces her thoughts across the page,
and looks forward to
the longer nights of winter.

Trimesters

one

my mother in her bedroom
  slipping on a nightdress
her voice as thick as cream
  the muffled drum of her heart
and the streaming of bubbles through long narrow spaces

  lying on her back
head raised on pillows as if she is looking down on me
  despite the blankets
despite the dark
  despite her closed eyes

a story is already unfolding
  me face to face with the moon
remembering its cool tug
  my mother standing beside me
staring out at the stars

  she is dreaming a car trip
my father at the wheel
  her hand on his left leg
her thoughts threading him
  and the road's slow glow

her thoughts weave me too
  these delicate raw parts
binding me in her silences
  looping her dreams into knots
and tying them round me in beautiful chains

two

through my lids colours blush
as if embarrassed
to be seen smeared

somewhere so private;
I try out my lips, swallow
all remaining darkness;

my fists unfurl like peonies
touch the edges of light;
my mother's palm caresses her belly

its shadow like the faint gasp
at seeing up close the ghost
of some unknown ancestor;

she rubs in circles
trying to smooth out her childhood
so she can translate it

in the dark of her bed;
sometimes she thinks of her own mother
feels my kicks

wonders if they are reaching towards her
or away.

three

I who am being drawn
towards a new orbit,
towards a spill of milky stars
with which to seal my bones.

I who am cosmonaut
suspended in zero gravity
waiting for my turn
to touch the moon.

I who am atom
fused by quiet experiment
now with a life of its own
that could blow the world apart.

I who am the place where
all dark matter goes
to harden, become animal,
be transformed.

I who am beyond the horizon
watch the sun begin to rise,
hear paws padding closer
hungering for blood.

Sprinkler

At the crunch of tyres on gravel
we scramble, knees smarting, over
Mrs McLintoch's brick wall,
flip our sandals into flower beds,
flick the nozzle.

Scorched grass prickles our feet
so we hop and jitter
between the bleached patches,
daring each other
through the spray.

Get set! Go! — and we're flying,
a shriek of pink bikinis
through the silver dome
that frisks the sky, shivers
down on hot brown skin —

we are sharp as lemons,
slick as minnows,
we are slippery
seconds in the long slow weeks of a heat-wave
and no one can catch us —

over the rockery, the crack
of chuckies round papyrus
crawling with red mites
that squash under thumbs
into sly orange stains

and through the archway
I can spy from my bedroom window,
its trellis bound with scented jasmine,
the hush of its white lips
thick with secrets.

Seafaring

They slept in an ocean liner,
  a padded, studded headboard at the bow.
Straight across the hall from mine
  it gleamed like royalty.

Over there, my mother's dressing table:
  white, gilt-edged, a glass sheet over damask lace
on which hairbrush, comb and hand mirror
  nestled in velvet.

Here, my father's crumpled handkerchiefs,
  a scatter of battered paperbacks, bridge magazines,
the soft balls of yesterday's socks:
  a trove of sweat and grime.

Evenings he would return, raise the anchor,
  draw curtains over portholes
and tell me tales
  of the strange new worlds he'd seen.

Alone I'd creep across the purple pile,
  hold my balance against the sea's sway
and drape myself in silks,
  pearls and white high-heels.

Slipping in on Sunday mornings
  between the salty air and deep skin,
I'd lie awake listening
  for the creak of beams and planks

and the scuttling of galley rats.

Sleeping in Elephant Print Bedclothes

I never hear
his bookish tread nor feel
walls of warm air flapping
from the ragged edges of his ears.

He wears across his back
the secrets of the Thar,
an invisible howdah high above
the continent of his belly.

Sometimes I'll glimpse a foot
the girth of a tree-stump
retreating from the outer edges of
my subconscious plains,

or while arguing with a composite
of close family members
I'll see dusty-lashed eyes gazing
back at me with solemn curiosity.

Occasionally I awake
the next morning with a leaden head
and the strange sensation
that my nose was longer in the night,

so long that I could spray
the quenching waters of distant oases
over my parched desert skin
while playing in the sand with the antelope.

But most of the time he keeps
himself to himself
and the only sign of him on waking
is his footprint deep in my pillow.

Day of Rest

She skates through the house
collecting saucers and spoons
like pebbles from a frozen lake.

From tables to mantels her fingers flutter
while we slouch over the Sundays.

Sometimes the hum of Ravel's Bolero
can be heard above the vacuum's drone
or the dishwasher's drum-roll

as blade marks carve through the carpets, past
snow-drifts in forgotten corners;

and when we gather round the table,
her apron twirls as she turns
to serve our favourite roast

but no one has the grace to raise
a perfect 6.

Visiting Hours

I don't see you at first: a drift
of pastel cardigans, fading knits, sweet tea
and last year's magazines,
their quiet drivel.
In the corner you are sleeping,
hands folded on your lap,
head hinged back: a skull-shaped mask
haloed by silver.
Your eyes open, slow as a turtle,
paddling my face, its unfamiliar shapes,
swivelling the pieces
to try to make them fit.
I take your hand and your gaze hovers
— my own blue, my mother's blue —
sifting the hidden facts and seeing me now.
Sharon you smile and nod my palm up and
down and up and
down and
up and
down

Pescado

In a restaurant in Spain
you showed me how to dine on fish:

line up the body,
pierce the skin's grey slick,
pull the blade down the spine,
scrape the membrane's
thickening glaze.

Only then can a knife split
the neat flank, plough
flesh from bone
into a drift of perfect flakes.

Today I prepare trout,
scales sticking to my fingers,
bright as a wound,
and grill it *a la plancha*
in place of the sandwiches
they serve at your wake.

Heirloom

It's a process, not an object:
this slow unclipping of catches,
the raising of the dust case, the unveiling
of cast iron and polished steel.

Weekends I'd sit at your side, watch the unravelling
of cables, the way you guided colour
through intricate hooks and eyes,

worked the pedal with your stocking'd foot,
the cloth spreading and disappearing over the edge
as you drove the lockstitch forward.

Later, on its rare outings, I'd heave its weight
to your table, thread the needle
too small for failing sight, your frail hands moving deftly

in ways you knew by heart —
a complicity of shape, click, tug;
when to twist a dial, how to fix a slipping stitch.

Today it's the heaviest thing I own,
heavier even than my youngest child
who never saw you stem a fraying edge.
Sometimes I bring it out just to

slide aside the steel plate, run a duster
across its smooth buff length,
its brass insignia, unwind the wires
coiled around its girth

to give the hidden parts a chance to breathe.

First Litter

She birthed the first by a puddle
on the path, looked surprised

when I scooped it up, laid it gently
in the cushioned nest we had prepared.

The second, third and fourth appeared
without ado, moist as figs, lolling

in her thick brown fur, her tongue licking
their slick backs, sealed eyes,

tiny paws with claws like angel-hair,
the limp commas of their tails.

We watched her cup herself around them,
nudge them into life, her purr steady as milk,

pupils dilating as they squirmed,
latched on. Later she moved them

to a thread-worn blanket under our bed,
fetching them one by one across the warm pine floor.

I lie awake at night — your left arm slack
across my belly, mapping hollows,

your fingers draped against my hip
— and listen to them: the tiny mews, the break

and draw of suction, the hum of instinct
suckling in the dark.

After Skye
(b. 1999)

And you were born at that moment:
beneath Storr's peak you grew
raw as the bay, its mist, its crocheted shawls.

I felt you in my bones as the air
salted my tongue, your seed bedding down
like a word. Your name on my lips

was the sting of whisky, my grandfather's moustache,
blackberries scrumped at the farms of Mearns.
A wind was brewing,

the sea shedding its pelt
on the flesh-coloured sand
before cutting its feet on the rocks.

Eight years on you break my own waves,
shiny from sweat, vernix, brine;
the tiny squall of your body

fighting up my belly,
            mouth wide open, rooting
                        for the island of my breast.

Unborn

(after Iona)

It's how I pictured you:
marram-blond, naked of trees,
your fingers steeped in sand,

lying on a sea-blue blanket, swaddled
in soft grey clouds and sky,
joined to me by bedrock.

You were always going to be the gentle one.
Above the abbey, white pigeons
write your name in cursive script;

waves flutter high upon the beach,
all thoughts of blue suddenly interrupted;
lucid green pebbles shed themselves in the bay.

You came to me too late — me, the mainland,
already with whole civilisations to support,
my head was full of earth and clouds.

At the hospital they said your stone
had been warming for five weeks.
I swallowed pills; you washed away.

Today I leave you again, on the ferry to Mull —
in its wake, an umbilical cord of froth
connecting the islands —

and when I turn at Fionnphort you are
small enough to fit in my hand
as if you had simply floated to the surface,

as if you were simply sleeping on the horizon
of someone else's palm.

Contacts

I leave them floating in their case
snug as unborn twins
and wander out of the house, into the garden —

a mortal let loose in the world of the gods,
unshackled from the myth of edges,
each contour a shimmering aureole;

a lucid dreamer gliding through his reverie,
directing his cast
with the merest squint or narrowing of an eye.

Here, light is tipsy: photons careen towards the cornea,
race through the lens and stumble to the retina,
giddy and out of step.

It's an exercise in quantum physics —
each object a fizzing mass of particles
freed from our idea of it:

the forsythia hedge bulges like a mohair dragon,
the lawn is a knitted rug, the geraniums in their pots
are scarlet handprints.

Behind me the household wakes.
In the bathroom I untwist the two white caps
— Logic and Reason —

and like a well-meaning doctor
pop in the plastic
that will lead me through the day

with a score of 20/20 and within
clearly defined limits.

Motherland
(after a painting by Isis Olivier)

(i) Breakwater

In the middle of a gallery
I've wandered into to avoid the rain
in this smart Parisian *quartier,*
I find you wanton and dreaming,

reclining in the Firth of Clyde —
naked but for the Isle of Arran
knuckled across your right breast; the dark mole
of Ailsa Craig midway down your *linea alba;*

a faint track of scars marking
underwater contours;
a single score of latitude. Your belly skims
the Ayrshire coastline,

stretch marks catching in the sun
like silvery eels,
your pubic thatch a shoal of fish
tugging on the current.

Both nipples are adrift — one nudging
the genteel seaside town of Troon,
the other its own unmapped island, cocked
towards Kintyre.

Elbow thrown back
above your tipped-back head, fist
plunging the depths of Loch Fyne,
the Sound of Jura in your ears,

you hold back tides and wait,
warm as stone,
for rusting herring trawlers and the lonely nets
of wind-beaten fishermen.

(ii) Sepia

Hard to tell where body ends and land begins:
this coastline mapped in tendons and arteries,
in erogenous zones and birth marks,
your moon-curves pushing back landslide, bays and cliffs,
these wrinkled, flaking edges
that could crumble
like parchment in my hands.

(iii) **Strand**

You wear your body like a scroll —
your past laid out in nautical miles,
your present etched
with grid coordinates, latitude, place
names I've never heard of,
each muscle tensed, each sinew pushed
proud of Earth's crust, pectorals pulled
tight as a footbridge
I've been waiting on the other side of for years.

(iv) **The Muse**

I angle thumb against parchment, squint,
count the widths from breast to coast
to situate your heart.

I find it plum on Lady Isle —
an island off the Ayrshire coast,
uninhabited but for a lighthouse:
a platform built on buttresses
with an exterior stairwell.

Today it is a bird sanctuary
and (despite the lighthouse) a popular place
for recreational sailors to run aground.

(v) **Resting Place**

They're out there searching still.
I hear the whirr of helicopter blades,
the churn of speedboats
as my loved ones scan
these cliffs
while divers sweep their flashlights
like miniature lighthouses.

They will find no sailor here tonight.

For I have returned to peat, granite, brine.
Soon the Atlantic will flood my veins,
my outline will have risen
as a livid scar of coastline
and the dust of me will have slipped below sand.
I shift to make myself comfortable
as the tide sucks me flesh-wards.

Clearing up the Playroom

She will dream tonight
of broken bits of Playmobil,
runaway wheels the size of millstones
and jigsaw pieces shrouded
from under the piano.
She will wake at midnight in a sweat.
In a collage of this day
she would paste all of the above
plus fluff-balls worn as evening gowns
by bald Barbies with missing limbs
and a wooden train track
scrawled with graffiti.
She would fix in the corners
coloured beads and knots of wool
and smear a flatline of glue
along the top with which to stick
painted plywood letters reading
I was once.
She would scatter
two dustpans of glitter and sequins
to complete the picture
and at the bottom she would sign her name
and gum a stray doll's head,
eyes glassy, staring at the wall.

Twelfth Day

The day we pack away the tree,
I almost vacuum her up —

which might explain the peg-arms thrust out front,
the startled pinpricks of her eyes —

when my attention is snagged
by a glint of wings: flimsy triangles outstretched

against the suction, braced
at the gates of my Hoover head.

I pick her up by the loop of thread sprouting
from her cranium — a thought bubble muted

by stupefaction — and consider
the fate so narrowly escaped:

clatter of arms and wings inside plastic tubing,
choke of warm air, hail of hardware,

before landing in a lungful of dust and grime;
cat hairs, crumbs, carpet fluff

and 90% human epidermis
to cushion her fall;

a celestial glow in my family's skin,
a deliverance so unholy she might

have clasped her hands and prayed.

Onset

Everything is as it was yesterday:
the blurred moon of her face in the mirror,
hair still slurred from sleep,

hands folding cold water as her lenses slide
into place,
light pooling on porcelain.

She looks at the brushes
splayed like flowers in their pot
and hesitates.

                    Her synapses snap
to red alert to test for chinks, rewind
the thread, but it's drifted like a sky-coloured bird.

In her hand the toothpaste,
cap unscrewed, the pearl of its head
splintered with red.

She remembers a barber shop,
the striped pole twisting in the sun —
like humbugs, her grandfather had said

his rheumy eyes squinting —
in his confusion he'd even asked
for a poke of pear drops instead of a haircut.

She weighs the ballast of her stomach
and picks the pink;
its bristles are rough, too rough on her tongue

so she pushes them to the back of her mouth
fixing on the mirror, fixing
on the froth over-spilling her lips.

Fibonacci Takes a Walk to Clear His Head

The question spirals down his throat

and lodges in his ribcage.

It is conch, a flowering artichoke,
a cochlea that hears only pulse.

It speaks a seaborne dialect. It speaks
of gases compressing, of stars
seeding like sunflowers, of the origin of salt.

It speaks of the trails of ancestors
dragging themselves from the surf;
a shedding of fins, scales, monocular vision.
The question turns again
and hooks in deep.

As he wanders the cathedral gardens of Pisa
he sees it in everything.
The tower straining for it. He feels
its pressure when he inhales:
a bruise, a colour breathing into life,
the small ache
of coming back to himself
while spinning   further away.

Snipe

He fires words across the table;
they lodge like shot

in the feathers of her neck.
She picks them out one by one

and tries to link them into sentences,
rearrange them into something she can use.

Her shoulders ache
as if something has been clipped from them

but she can't remember what,
only that these days the light

seems to weigh her down
and her thoughts stream like bubbles
                                    just out of reach.

It's been so long since she touched water
she has forgotten its name,

its cool breath on her belly,
the way it carries the larch, cedar, yew

in susurrant meditation.
Her fork nudges the pale

meat he has served her
from which she extracts a slug of lead.

It slips through her fingers,
poisonous and cold as an eye.

Walking on Eggshells

You can do it providing
you set them out carefully,
tapered ends up.

You should wear plimsolls;
there must be no excuse
for noise.

Exhale steady poles of light
through your fingertips
then step lightly from one peak to the next

with a tight-rope walker's concentration.
If you're lucky you will make it
to the other side of that day's clutch

spread out like a knuckle that stretches for miles
from one room to the next.
If you slip —

hold perfectly still while the ground
cracks open like a skull;
fall as discreetly as possible

into the sudden roar
of albumen, blood, yolk,
of thin limbs and unopened wings;

hold your breath against the stench
of all that's rotten and raw
and pray, just pray, that this time

you'll land on feathers.

Autopsy

I gave you my tongue
right back to my throat,
I had no more need for it
with yours in my mouth.

I offered you my bones
smooth as the moon,
clattering in the hemp sack
you carried them home in.

You smiled to see my gut
cleaned and laid out before you
like a tapeworm
still twitching, still sucking for food.

I passed you the bandage of my skin
unpeeled like a fruit;
you thrilled at the unbroken ribbon,
called me your Nefertiti.

I gave you my blood
from my wrists, from between my legs,
from the slash across my belly
where my organs slithered out.

Now you have left I leave you
my shadow: distilled,
scrawled on paper,
sealed with my lips.

Morning After

She arches back as far as she can reach;
her throat is a pale bridge stretching
from her chest to the moon. Her fingers ache

from touching him; the veins
on the back of her hand protrude like twine,
unravelled, almost frayed. She fingers

his outline, tastes his salt, her tongue
tightening.
Among the creases she finds a hair;

held to the square light of day
it bends from her like bulrush
caught in a squall.

She draws the sheets around her like tissue,
balls them close as if to protect
something fragile, something about to

slip from its wrapper.

Cowcaddens

(i) Circling

She spends her days
   in their flat above The Gala
listening for his tread,
   pacing the worn Kashmiri carpet,
twisting the gold band
   round her finger.

It circles her henna-painted skin,
   the red knuckle
of a life led in-waiting;
   it circles her flesh
like a hawk, like a dog
   chasing its tail,

like the hands of the clock
   above her kitchen sink,
like the moon, *Chandra,*
   that keeps its distance
while roulette balls below her feet
   narrow their target

in ever-decreasing circles
   and everyone stands
an equal chance.

(ii) **Shopping**

Six months in Scotland and her sari's lost
its scorched scent of spices:

star anise in open baskets,
cardamom pods crushed into
pots of steaming *chai*,

plumes of cumin-tinged smoke
rising from the chapattis spun thin
by crouching women.

The coloured silks brushing her ankles
are rain-smeared, grey

as she makes her way
to Chadni's Cash'n'Carry.

She's fading from the outside in.

(iii) **Air Mail**

She struggles to understand
the man behind glass
pushing the parcel back to her.
His words rush like a monsoon through slums,
churning silt and mud
until she feels she's drowning.

Please, madad karo, she says,
the phrase trickling over her lip
like the holy water at Tungnath temple.

But he doesn't help —
waves her on, shaking his head
as another customer pushes past.
A poster of stamps reads
Birds of the World,
each depicting outstretched wings —

she thinks of ioras swooping and diving
above her village shrine where she used to lay
sweetened *laddu,* rose petals.

In Her House

time comes bottled
in phials, in ornamental flasks.

They twinkle on the shelves
like miniature glass Buddhas;

her fingers long to skim
their taut, cool bellies.

Hunched over housework
she glances across at them, biding.

Alone, she unstraps her watch
and uncorks a stopper,

splashes her bare limbs and
rubs her feet, their callused skin —

the clock dozes to a halt, its numbers
like juggling balls suspended in mid-air

as she stretches out,
an unhooked pendulum,

soaking up minutes and hours
in the sun's puddle

then replaces the lid like a thief
and licks her fingers clean.

When he returns her hands are deep in suds.
Parched, he pours himself whisky or wine.

Storytelling

I want to own books that bear the marks
of the readers they have owned:

pages dog-eared at the corners where sleep
folded one day into the next,

the raised arm of an exclamation,
a passage underlined,

marginal notes scrawled like starlings
in a strip of cloudless sky.

My books should flaunt their influence,
wear emotions on their sleeve:

a spine etched deep with wrinkles, bound
with threads like broken veins,

a tidemark where bathwater crept
and carried off a thought bubble,

coffee stains and nicotine,
the imprint of a mug.

So take this tattered paperback,
disappear within it, please,

and later I will read you, track you
down between the lines,

hold the ghost of you, undisturbed
by chapters, heroes, plot;

I'll listen to the stories whispered
from among its soiled sheets,

revealing parts of you more intimate
than any cheap confessional,

any lover's words.

Palomas

He ekes words from the colour of the soil,
from the reek of sixty days of piss, shit, sweat;
from his knowledge of each man's breath, the tension
at the earth's heart.

He writes his letters by the alchemy of truck batteries,
tucks them gently as eggs
into the abdomens of white *palomas:*
news to hatch in his family's hands.

He tells how he's forgotten blue —
the wink of *el Salar de Llamara;*
the muscled flinch of swordfish;
a lone star, fading. How he knows

morning only from his wristwatch,
from the sudden stringed fluorescence at 6am,
from his daily ration
of half a spoon of tuna, one biscuit, a mouthful of milk.

He holds his notebook upside down,
lets the sheets fall open like wings:
a pair for every man down here,
he must leave no page empty.

*Note: In 2010, thirty-three Chilean miners were trapped for 69 days. Victor Zamora,
a mechanic, sent his wife poems in plastic capsules nicknamed palomas ("doves"). The
Chilean flag is known as la Estrella Solitaria ("the lone star").*

Lune

(i) Asylum

They storm their fists on the walls
rattle the windows
and hurl thunderbolts
at the blind eye of the moon
hanging from its socket
until the nurses come running
slide silver into their arms
and fill their veins
with stardust.

(ii) Hysteria

After she is seized behind
the Barras Ballroom
with her lover in her arms
they strap her down, force-
feed her pills of mercury
set leeches on her scalp
and plunge her into icy water
to stop the wandering.

But as the chiffon clouds slide
from the moon's polished lens
her heart begins to clack like spoons
her lungs begin to drone like pipes
and they cannot stop
they cannot stop her
womb from dancing.

House of Swan

You strike
and I flare inside a cage of ice,
dance the dance you taught me as a cygnet
when you made me walk across your cigarette's flicked ash.

Too narrow for the spread of wings
but wide enough to gaze for hours at my reflection
as bones fuse into shapes too tight
for normal flight.

I am older now.
The ice has melted, I glide on water;
have pledged myself to a different mirror image
and built a nest of softest down.

Yet still you strike
your words against me,
still the flame burns bright

while underneath these feathers
my skin sings for you,
black as char.

No Magician

I cannot sketch these walls in colour,
   paint reflections into household things,
transform your pale fingers
   into exotic dancers
across the stage of the breakfast table.

I cannot cut holes in your silences,
   turn them into star-shaped flakes
like paper doily decorations,
   line your windows with them,
hang them in the naked trees.

I cannot sew beads into the sky,
   embroider a moon from silver threads
to turn your view into
   something more than simply winter;
I cannot pull bright silks from my sleeve.

I have only this threadbare jacket,
   its pockets filled with words,
all of them white rabbits,
   all of them hopping
            invisibly
                  into the
                        snow.

Slipknot

My head is the room where they found you.
The floorboards speak in whispers
and through mottled windows, birds twitch
on broken boughs.

All week I've watched you, slowly twisting.
Downstairs a door rattles, a frame creaks.
The sun smiles weakly and stretches across the table
to your note, folded
neat as a handkerchief in a top pocket.

No one has arrived yet to untie you.
The only visitors are feral cats
that stalk these shadows,
lift their noses, glimpse your ankles, scatter.
I can't sleep at night from the stench.

*

I pop a paracetamol to cool my skull.
In bed, my husband's arm lies
in a crook around his head,
his hot breath catching every third stroke of the clock.

I dream of white flowers
thrown in the ground.

*

And when the rain comes, they are still
filling the hole; brown clods
clinging to spades,
topsoil collapsing.

The path is too narrow for our seethe of bodies;
our umbrellas are sudden blooms on the hillside
as we burst down the slope
in a daze of nylon.

*

Warm white wine and sandwiches
served with slow handshakes, low murmurs
and foggy memories picked out by headlights of grief.

In a corner your mother rocks
to the din of crashing plates,
her eyes are filled with crumbs.

Back along the track,
a thin silhouette in the drizzle
polishes the tombstone.

*

For five days now the white chrysanthemum
I picked from the dirt has survived.
Suspended in water,
its petals are loosening, its whorl is slack
as a mouth.

Still Life in the Pennines

Up by Janet's Foss a felled beech
sprawls from stream to footpath,
its twisted branches patched with lichen,
trunk bejewelled from rings to tip:

copper and nickel pennies, brass centimes
slotted in the soft, damp wood
or hammered into cracks, some bent
flush against the grain.

It's a crocodile slithered from the shallows;
a beast with fish-scales soldered
from a sunken pirate stash; a mica mass
of tadpoles wriggling upstream.

Or a fallen soldier who'd just stretched out
to quench his thirst
when the axe struck from behind —

his dignity restored in chainmail
glinting in the sun, he is
a tributary heading into battle
where xylem and phloem used to march.

Brocken Spectre

He said he saw one once on Crib Goch ridge:
a shadow rising from the corrie,
an oracle on a stage of clouds.
A chill uncoiled around his neck as he rooted

his feet in the heather, reaching
for the thread stitched
across Snowdon's peak to steady himself.
And each time he turned

it turned with him, its halo catching in the sun:
one hand raised in greeting,
two raised in surrender —
like a photo negative, like

a Rorschach blot anchored in the wind,
like that day the surgeon
pinned his scan before him
giving him twelve months, eighteen tops.

Note: a Brocken spectre is a large shadowy figure that appears when looking down into mist from a ridge or peak with a low sun behind the climber. The head is often surrounded by glowing rings or coloured light caused by the refraction of water droplets.

Counselling

You kneel in the garden of us,
push your hands in deep
and scrape out a hole.

The bulbs go in like candles;
you cover them over and pat them down
preparing a bed that will blaze all summer.

You separate last year's rhizomes,
splitting them cleanly,
their multiplied growth.

You tease apart root-balls,
unravel their threads, clip the tips,
settle them back in the soil

then tilt your can, wash the dirt from your hands
and pass it to me. Overhead, clouds nudge
a new moon rising in the stark March sky.

I breathe in the blowzy pollen,
sharp as Round-Up.

Sabotage

I want to capture the spirit of you
    hold it down gently
trace its contours in soft lead
    to frame by my bed.

I want to record its smallest sounds
    lean my microphone in close
to catch its blips and scratchings
    over the amplified hiss.

I want to swaddle it in cotton
    warm it in my pocket
pull it out in the sudden swoon of day
    like smelling salts.

I want to feel it struggle in my fist
    to know its strengths, its limits
the precise moment
    at which it begs for air.

I want to gather the tiny bruises on my palm
    the bite marks on my fingers
that I will pick and pick
    into a permanent scar.

I want to grind its wings
    to a gleaming powder
to hang in a locket
    around my neck.

I want to whisper
    that everything will be all right
that it has no need to lie here trembling
    that the pin in my hand is just to hold it

nice and steady.

Crackling

He is going to leave me.

The certainty lies
like a dead animal in the cave
of your stomach.

You prepare the dinner table,
laying out your best cutlery,
the red tapered candles.

You pull the cork, set the wine to breathe:
a Burgundy, dark as split berries.

*

He will be here soon.

The chicken will be perfect —
tender as your flesh was once
under his tongue,
white veils parting at his touch,
effortless as falling backwards
— his favourite dish.

You draw the knife, satisfied:
the juice runs clear and sweet.

*

Nothing will spoil this evening, nothing.

A car hums in the drive, an engine cuts.
You press colour to the centre of your lower lip.
Check your smile.
Adjust your neckline.
Feel the cool drip
of your pendant between your breasts.

*

He is wearing a new cologne.

He kisses your cheek, does not see
the crack behind your eyes.

In the kitchen you pinch foil
around the swollen chest
— crisp, honey-glazed —
lick your fingers,
set the carving knife aside
for later.

Binge

she gulps peach slices and   tinned pears
cured meats and   memories   preserved in brine
     she gulps Jaffa Cakes
   and slabs of   processed   solitude

she is in a lavatory
in a cold room
on her lunch break
at six minutes past one

she does it quietly, steadily
because no one's told her to
because it weighs her like ballast
because it fits like a straitjacket

it tastes of   habit,
   of   sugared almonds,
     of sleeping pills
  and warm milk

     of something that once flowed abundantly
but she kept to herself
like a fresh cut.

Scoring

We play Scrabble by an open fire
in a hotel room far from home;
a tangle of words ring
the double score at the centre.

Our points creep up side by side.

Years have passed since the night
you flouted the rules,
returning home with her smell on your neck,
apologies clacking like a bag of letters.

We are older now and wiser, you say.

You play *trial* for 14 points
(triple letter, double word);
I use my whole hand on *sentence* for 80
(double word, 50 bonus points).

I break my own record, leaving you
to gather the pieces.

Learning to Swim

No alarm is required
to break the moon of my sleep:
this sea splits without effort,
without anyone's help.

The act of eating must come first
then bathroom matters,
feet slicing the current
to stay afloat.

Keys. Car. Post box. Shop.

High tide floods these shores
at the cast of each greeting.
My replies are the skins of fish;
make, break eye contact,

fold my hands over all wounds,
tread water, tread water,
above all, smile —
these things too I must tick off the list.

I remember now.
This is how they said it would be
away from the ocean floor.

Will-o'-the-Wisp

It drifts in late when I'm asleep
disturbs the shadows
traces luminous maps on my back

of the places it has been: in my dreams
it is fathoms deep
its fingers under the covers

are the sway of cord grass
at the fringe of a marsh; sometimes
I sense it on waking like a brackish stain in the air

I swallow its incantation
but by dusk it is almost forgotten;
only when undressing

do I notice the trail of stars down my spine
the constellations on my thighs
the taste of salt on my cracked lips

and I find you kneeling before me, reaching out in the half-light
soaked to your waist
with no idea how you got here.

Travelling the Dadès Valley

Out of the foothills — the High Atlas peaks just a blue
pencil sketch behind us — the land yawns towards Djebel Saghro,
pink and mauve ridges scumble the sky.

Kasbahs rise like giant sandcastles from the dust;
palm oases are verdelite butterflies
touching down to drink.

Donkeys piston through the heat
under sagging sacks of mint, wheat, barley —
or graze at the margins, their ankles tethered to sepia.

We follow the ink line of the road
past red knuckles of cliff, a finger-gouged gorge, houses etched
into rock-face, swatches of fig trees and almonds —

until the canvas splits its frame, rolls out
like parchment and we slide towards the dunes of Erg Chebbi:
globs of ochre awaiting the finest sable brush.

Djemaa el Fna, Marrakech, April 2011

After the *derbs*: a gold-flecked labyrinth
of shuffling *jalabas*, donkeys, handcarts, kebab
vendors, open doorways stuffed with coloured scarves,
babouches, spice pyramids, pomegranates —
the souk spits us out like pips into the main square

where bongos fibrillate the air; stalls slump
under wreaths of dried figs and oranges; a man
with a monkey minces, palm outstretched,
among tie-dyed travelers —
slick as snake oil, a hooded charmer slaloms

across to where I stand, a python head-locked
between his thumb and forefinger; presses its neck
to my forehead, cheeks, belly, bestowing blessings;
presses the bowl of his hand to my chest
for *dirham, dirham!* — a woman flickers

at my side, a dart of henna in her fist, grabs
my daughter's hand and scrawls
a calligraphy of swirls — her fingers working deftly
over the fleshy canvas, pumping ochre
up her wrist, over the fine bones of her fist —

before I can even object she's onto my other daughter,
the snake man is trying to shake
her off, gabbling in Arabic —
but she avoids eye contact, shrilling
objections, the nib darting from knuckle to fingertip

in patterns that will wash off to leave an orange stain
as cryptic and pre-meditated as this city
and the bomb that went off five days later.

Love Note, Erg Chebbi

We see them in the valley of the dunes:
wind-whipped circles in the sun
like locks of lovers' hair; wedding rings; keepsakes;
concentric kisses blown across the sand.
Last night's wind bowed
the grasses' heads, nib to canvas,
to draw a hundred hushed perimeters:
Venn diagrams in which lives are spheres that intersect
in all possible versions of themselves
to create perfect ellipses
beyond the scarab beetles and dromedary scat.

The Gift

This heart is desert marble
scored with tracks
of camel, gecko, rattlesnake.

You place it on my pillow every night:
a gift offered at the border of sleep
like a passport or a bribe.

It is cool in my hand,
heavy as a promise. I try to match
my palm lines to its paths:

some, frayed knots that loop
back to the start;
others striking a straight course to the tip before veering

away, petering out
like a traveller, parched and belligerent.
Only one path bridges the gulf

between stone and flesh —
        leaping clear
of the blunted point and running head-first into my lifeline.

Celestial Bodies

(i) Cosmonaut

You wear the moon like a glove
that has been draped over the back
of my mind all day. You wear it
so well, I don't even feel your hand
sliding over, into, through me —
as if I were the ghost of your beloved
grandmother, your hell-bent cousin
with the beautiful singing voice,
your mute maiden aunt who died
wearing only *mousquetaires*
after slipping from her window
one bright, sloping night.

(ii) Supernova

and when you slant across my belly
and a sister-pulse flutters
deep in my groin,
I breathe in the stars, loosen
their constellations in my mouth
and balance their orbits
on the tip of my tongue,
to stop myself

(iii) **Nebula**

The hours steal away, some
unlatching the shutters, spreading
their wings in the cool air;
some through cracks in lath and plaster;
some riding out on white horses —
bold as the moon, and shining.

(iii) **Eclipse**

and later, when you lift
your body from mine
and drift into the night,
I wrap myself in your shadow,
layering it round me
tighter and tighter
until I all but disappear

The First Cup

Stiff and woolly-headed, I roll
from bed. Already it infuses everything:
I shower under kettle-hot water,
towel myself with sachet-thin cotton.

You serve me toast and orange juice
but the tea I make myself — tapping
out the pinched green balls, pouring
boiling water to the brim

then watching as they slowly bloom,
uncurl, their edges overlapping,
one pale leaf-stalk nudging another's
unclenched fist as it reaches up for air.

It's an orgy of green: smoky-moss-weed-green
loosened to decadence, seeping chlorophyll.
A bubble feels its way along a leaf vein.
Steam plumes in the kitchen's cool breath.

I wait until the colour's almost sepia,
till morning's angles are bowed in reverence;
minutes evaporate, edging my cup
in beads of precipitation.

The first sip is pure light, white composed
of every spectrum hue; Chinese women
harvesting fields in vivid *hanfu*
with baskets on their backs, women

strong as honey against a copper sun,
their faces like lanterns strung across the dawn.

Siesta

Lizards line the lintels;
cats stretch out like pelts
to sip at pockets of shade,
too tired to twitch at passing flies.

Your coiled body gilds our bed
as our sweat drifts, pungent, mingling;
my foot in your hand
glistens like clay.

The clock's second hand
trails like a stick along park railings
collecting the minutes and hours;

spiders slouch in silk cradles
among the whitewashed beams,
their bodies fat on flies;

through the open window,
the spark of cicadas, legs like tinder
that could set this afternoon alight.

Your green eyes flicker over me
like freshwater pools,
quenching my thirst
as we sprawl on this crumpled canvas like a Klimt.

Dharma

These mountains are Buddhas, recumbent
on tatamis of woven rush
laid out across the temple of this valley
under a hand-painted ceiling of blue.

Our home, a fold in this one's robe;
that cloud, a handkerchief drifted from his pocket;
even the bees drone to a slumber
as they waft in on his breath.

His brow is smooth as a prayer flag,
his belly shimmers in the heat.
He is dreaming cicada and birdsong.

West Highland Line

Out of Garelochhead and over Rannoch Moor
the train rattles and creaks,
each turn eliciting a hydraulic gasp
as another loch or stubbled glen slides by.

*

Through a loom of trees, a doe and stag:
the female with her back turned,
her white rump an inverted heart;
the male in profile, still as a breath.

*

A copse of birch and alder:
jewellery trees on my mother's dressing table,
last night's rain draped along their branches,
the sun suspended
on their many hooks and forks.

*

The clouds are heron-grey.
A statue of the bird stands
on Dalmally platform, throat thrust out
as if in thrall at the thought
of one last flight.
Drizzle dampens its beak, its plinth,
the station's concrete slabs.

Above, the sky is softening,
its wings are spreading wide.

*

The loch snakes through slopes and dales,
shedding its silvery skin;
somewhere up ahead
a raw-backed creature
loses itself in the tussocky grass.

Cairn

(for Neil)

He greets each mountain as if it were a book,
strides out upon the first page with
his arms spread like an offering.

Across heather, haw and broom
a story prints itself,
his feet invent a pulse.

He reads defiance in granite,
sorrow in the schism of schist,
loss in the crumbling ledges of lime;

he reads tenderness in all that's yet to flower,
fills each dry riverbed with syllables
that spring from his mouth.

And each time something rises in him,
he sets it down in the mist
around his feet,

blinks back the dazzle of light
but he never stops walking —
the title lies just out of reach.

At the summit he bends to pick
a fallen word,
sets it high upon the cairn, tilts forward and waits

for the wind to steal his breath away.

High Tide

You meet me under a full moon,
dangerous as a spell, circling me
like a finger, coating me in your salt.

No words are exchanged as you read
the braille of my skin, my breath breaking
on whispering rocks, until

I lose myself in the white threads
of your eddies rising, falling
about my breasts, nipples hard as shells.

If I yielded to your tides you would draw me,
suck me, until my own swell would
crash and flood —

afterwards I'd float on my back —
like balsa, bleached, rubbed soft by sand —
seaweed in my hair — and drift towards the open sea.

You shimmer, daring me to dive,
shivers spiralling like silk
            about my shoulders,
                        about my neck.

Sea Glass

He spends his days sifting pebbles,
rough hands separating
bladderwrack from driftwood;
holds each piece to the light,
runs his thumb around its edges,
smooth as polished nails.

He collects them all — moss-green, ice-blue,
opaque as pearls, lucent as fish —
drops them in his pocket, counts each chink.

They settle in the darkness like eyes,
nudge his groin
through the coarse cotton lining.
Their shift and chime
echo his step, the sough of the sea
as he crosses the shore.

Later he sets them in rows
like mermaid scales
or a colour chart for frost.

Bunker

(after *Tube Shelter Perspective*, 1941, by Henry Moore)

My boy is sleeping now, his warm breath
lapping on my chest. I shift

on concrete, pull the blanket up around our necks,
my feet away from cold steel rails

that stretch into a deeper black than here.
Nothing to tell the night from day

except the stilted sway of sleep,
the hush of intimacies, and in the distance

a mother's voice riding the tide:
bye baby bunting, daddy's gone a-hunting...

There's comfort in these strangers,
pressed together like hands in prayer

below the streets of London. I rock
the plumb weight in my arms

and think of planes whining
through the shell-shocked city sky:

within each cockpit, a young man
with a girl back home, in whose plumpness

he longs to sink, to dream
of days as bright and rare as oranges.

Islands
(after Iona)

(i) Brim

This island is a footprint
on a carpet of cobalt, cyan and black
rolled out in ceremony across the Atlantic.

At first you think you're on the edge of the world —

but looking west across slate-grey it dawns
that edge is layered upon edge,
light upon light, blue upon blue.

(ii) Green Stones

There are connections everywhere —

the sinew stretching in the ferry's wake,
the gulls and curlews composing the sky
joining frontiers and shores in search of food

— and our hungering for something
not-yet seen, like the green stones I've heard
exist at Columba's Bay,

the elusive corncrake, a silence
filled with calls of birds, sheep, wind
and the small, familiar achings of the waves.

(iii) Columba's Bay

The tides rise and fall and rise again,
gaining and losing inches, revealing
this bay of pink and turquoise pebbles

and creamy white sand, as if the sea
were an engorged mother
emptying herself into the mouth of her young.

(iv) Deliverance

The heart may be an island but the sea
brings in its memories —
          the curve and call of ships,
the soft belly and jabbing beak of tern, curlew, gull,
          freshwater springs, the rusting bones
and dreams of fishermen — all are laid on our shores.

Mornings I comb the beach to feel their pulse.

Climbing Dun I

A path that blackens to bog
and runoff and sheep-drop scree;

elbows and fists of granite and gneiss;
unbroken blue at our backs, flashes

of turquoise, white ribbons
hemming the sea; below

the blackest sheep we've ever seen
like ink drops spattered on a page;

yesterday's awkward boulders reduced
to a grey fleece of coastline;

smooth machair thumbing gently in
from the dunes and foaming ebb;

ears whistling with the cold but our bodies
warm as kettles under our jackets;

and finally this cairn held fast
against the wind's wild tides,

the toss and keel of battened clouds
and the sky's bright anchorage.

Fingal's Cave

Staffa is the grinning mouth
of a whale. Our boat edges in
through a knocked tooth, on a tongue of sea
— we admire its glottis, its palate,
its idle breath.

And later as we sit Jonah-like
on basalt dentistry,
our heads raised towards a guano fresco
on the ceiling, we hear it:

an echo of Mendelssohn,
the drone of a church organ
as if the island were calling us to prayer.

Mouche Volante

It slides and jerks at the shift of your eye. Skirts
the edges of your gaze. Absorbed

in the view, or obscured by your mental
leaps, it rarely hooks your attention

as it sinks, drifting downstream
until tugged by an invisible line.

Behind closed lids under a bright sky you toy with it:
look to the right and it's a hare in action;

to the left and it's a toddler on a tiny tricycle,
pedalling to keep up. You hold it still

by concentrating just beyond its perimeter,
skewering it to the spot, before

nudging it along the tropics of your globe
with minute quivers of your ocular muscle.

By your bedside lamp you excavate its outline
— skinny rectangle, capped head —

and picture it when asleep: in REM
swimming Olympic-style from one side of your eyeball

to the other — until settling, dropping
exhausted to the silt of its bowl as you wake.

Cactus

You punch the air, spikes thrust upwards
like some leathery punk;
if you could, you'd have LOVE and HATE
tattooed on each tubercle.
Day after day fails to reach you;
only the faintest fluctuations of temperature
stir your skin as a door opens,
coals are lit and extinguished,
footsteps unsettle the air.
Up close you are exotic monotony.
tough as old Mexican boots.
I won't breathe a word of how,
from the armchair at the room's far side
glimpsed against the skyline,

you are a lotus, unanchored.

Fathoms

I sit on the jetty, cast my line into silence;
first directly below my feet,
later into eddies.

Hours pass; a tug: the water opens like a flower
petals scattering
and I'm yanking light —

Look! a bright blue word
thrashing its silver belly,
the thick set of its mouth turning over and over —

like a lapis amulet,
like a sky, uninterrupted;
although on closer inspection I see

it is a tongue
deprived of oxygen, quivering.

*

A doctor presses a wooden spatula
into my mouth. *Aahhh* I obey
and whole seas spill out.

His expression is serious. There are islands
queuing at the back of my throat,
several miles of reef

and a raft-load of sailors
in soiled clothes, half-starved,
who haven't seen a woman in weeks.

In a nearby cove, humpbacks surface like phrases.
The sailors haven't seen them yet
but have stumbled upon a coconut tree
and a freshwater source.

*

The doctor's frown is a familiar scribble
as he replaces his spectacles
and hands me the prescription;

it is crisp as salt crust,
his writing like seaweed,
his signature a tangle of net.

I nod like a goby behind glass,
rise through a jet stream of bubbles,
burst through the page.

Chinks

(i) Space

She mounts the slide on white fluorescence.
My breast is a galaxy, a freeze-framed swirl
of gas clouds and asteroids, orbiting on black.

I'm drawn to a constellation
gleaming at the edge, a cluster of stars
as perfect as the Pleiades.

Micro-calcifications, very suspicious,
we'll need to take a look; she taps
her finger into outer space

explaining the biopsy will extract
a sample of cells, a painless procedure
requiring only local anaesthetic —

but I barely hear her for the din
of silence as I float   without a spacesuit
                                        light years away.

(ii) Soft Fruit

She spreads her fingers in a V
across her own clothed breast,

angles them wide to show the segment
she will slice from mine —

a fruit quartered to the quick
to expel the slippery pips,

these seeds that fall without trace
to spread their inscrutable roots.

(iii) **Parking**

Two scars, she traces a line
from nipple to armpit, another down my axilla,
maybe three, circling my nipple,

to reshape the breast.
Through undrawn blinds I watch
a white car trying to park, indicator flashing

then reversing,   looping
        the roundabout, taking off
down the same jammed aisle —

carving a trail through the hospital car-park,
                                a jagged trajectory
                nobody knows of
except for the driver and me.

(iv) **Pre-Admission**

Buddha has shifted on the horizon.
From this new place his outline is askew,
he is simply a mountain to climb —

a breast-shaped crest, aureole to the clouds,
ridged with chinks, with clefts and dimples,
paths etched into red earth, shelves crumbling.

Beyond, lavender skies and a view
into the *Vallée Française*
with its clear green *Gardon* flowing south.

I plan my route. Shadows will be my footholds.
Along with stove, canvas, rope and hunting knife,
I pack a change of clothes.

A swimsuit for the other side.

(v) **The Waiting Room**

By the water cooler
two non-flowering plants protrude

from pebbles. Hard
to tell if they're real

or replicas, though one is tilted
towards a closed velux

the suggestion of an outside world.
Temperature-controlled air angles

into nose and mouth.
A nurse emerges, calls a name.
We shift on pink plastic, clutching doctor's notes

and wait our turn, try to bury our thoughts
in *Elle*, paperbacks, a Filofax,
to tamp them down with the weight of words
until they cannot breathe at all.

(vi) **Sprig**

Knowing I don't like flowers
you bring me olive — a single stem,
its leaves flung wide like arms:
topside jade-green, underside silver;
the whole divided by a central cicatrix.
I forget to put it in water. Next day it is still
turgid, still leathery in my hands
(flowers would be dead by now).
I trace the split fibres where you pulled it,
each ragged, sun-stopped filament,
and place it in a glass carafe
they bring at lunch
then set it on my bed-tray as a peace offering
to whichever god I have offended.

(vii) **And Strap Them to the Slab**
    (for Lucy)

Take steel laid out on steel. Take moulded plastic.
Take tools that scrape and pierce and slice
and suck out soft tissue as if it were fish eyes.
Take glass plates that draw together softly-softly
until a pressure-sensor withholds the final crush.
Take needles and hooks pushed in hard
behind places reserved for lovers.

Take what they are doing to my friend
who has it worse than me.
Take the white flag raised in the morning
and the red flag in the afternoon
so she's cocked all day, a loaded barrel
with trigger-happy tear ducts.

Take the touch of latex.
Take the slickness of doctors and rehearsed restraint.
Take checklists and choices and everything
patient-empowering.

Take the words they use —
metastasize, remission, infiltration.

Take the letter C —
a careful incision,
a carved parabola
that strives to
but will never be
an O.

(viii) **Breach**

The night before surgery, the river bursts its banks
and the pressure that's been building up for weeks
                                        spills forth.

All night long the water rants,   untethered,
                        foaming at the mouth, pounding dykes
as chunks of concrete flush downstream.

Slowly news comes in. Villages are flooded, fishing huts
and logging camps are gone, the pier ten miles from here has snap-
ped in two.

The current — that nudged ashore our raft all summer long
                        — is churning splinters, scattering
        detritus in its wake.

At 5am it enters the sea's glittering eye,
the salt tide spreading wide the choke of silt
                                        across the pewter bay.

This is where we fetch up, the lucky ones —
under a red-stained sky;
foam receding, bubbles drying on the sand.

(ix) **Navigation**

She scores my breast in black felt tip:
X marks the spot —

as if my body were a treasure map
where a buccaneer could flip his fortune
with a stash of diamonds, rubies, bullion.

Or, arriving too late, unearth
rocks, coal, fool's gold
with which to fill his pockets

before leaping from a flapping
skull and crossbones
                            into sapphires.

*

Daubing India ink, she pricks
my breast three times —
nipple, scar, sternum:

beauty spots, she smiles.

Later I sponge away the blue stains
and examine it, my Bermuda Triangle:
a zone in the western North Atlantic
where anything, even pleasure cruisers

can disappear.

*

Every day I break the line
of infrared, take up my position —
knees raised, arm stirruped above
my head, head keeled left.

A motor whirrs and I'm fed
backwards into a red objective;
reflected in the glass plate: my breast
harpooned by light.

The buzzer strains and flashes, invisible darts
target the beached blubber
of my organ — numb, swollen, scarred —

as if it still showed signs of life.

(x) Conciliation

After an hour I stop talking aloud
to Holsteins and Swaledales, to chinks in limestone
and my body is a mare
I'm riding bare-back:
        half a ton of gleaming palomino,
rippling haunches, mane like wind, a gust of tail;
she slicks over dale, ticks on tarmac
as effortlessly as a heartbeat.
        She's Mustang-wild
but doesn't mind a rider on her back,
not even the winking weight
of this October morning —
        pheasant spilling from marshes,
velvet rattle of bulrush, the plunging ledge
of Malham Cove, its clints and grikes —
all are riding with me. I know she remembers
        the stumble, the fall, the sight of me
on my back — but as we surge below the silvery skin
of a sky untainted by clouds,
I clap her hard and silently assure her
        — and I know she understands —
that I never needed to forgive her,
no, I never needed to forgive her at all.

Anam Cara
(Gaelic: *soul friend*)

They are everyone and everything I meet
but I see them only when the weather's right,
when the storms of my heart
and the light rainfall of my head fall silent, and
the windsock of time hangs absolutely still —

as if a giant foot had eased itself free of it
after a steep climb
and lain down for a moment in the soft, long grass.

Pilgrimage

My journey is with the names of things;
words on a page.

Each one an island — an archipelago
of letters bound by sandbars
— anchored in a milk-white sea.

I climb them one by one to understand
their hearts. To know bedrock.

Equinox

All night she tracks the moon
through the mulch of sky,
watches it wick from feet to pelvis.

She lies as still as silver, offers
the banks of her body
for its consumption.

Beyond the window, night creatures
shuffle in the cut grass.

Soon it will be harvest.
High water. Howling leaves.

Appendix

'Fibonnaci Takes a Walk to Clear His Head' (previously entitled 'Fibonacci Ponders the Origin Of Life') won The Frogmore Prize 2011 and took 2nd prize in the Kent and Sussex Poetry Competition 2011

A version of 'Chinks' (previously entitled 'Breach') won *The New Writer* Competition 2010 (Poetry Collection category)

'After Skye' won *The New Writer* Competition 2009 (Single Poem category)

'Sabotage' was runner-up in Wigtown Book Festival Poetry Competition 2011

'The First Cup' won 2nd prize in Ilkley Literature Festival Poetry Competition 2010

'Palomas' won 2nd prize in *Agenda* Poetry Competition 2011

'Siesta' won 2nd prize in Grace Dieu Poetry Competition 2010

A collection of 10 poems took 2nd prize *The New Writer* Competition 2009 (Poetry Collection category)

'Storytelling' won 2nd prize in the EKO Poetry Competition 2009

'Sea Glass' won 3rd prize in the MAG Poetry Prize 2009

'Autopsy' won 3rd prize in *The New Writer* Competition 2010 (Single Poem category)

'Walking on Eggshells' and 'No Magician' were finalists in the *Aesthetica Creative Works* Competitions 2009 & 2010

'Snipe' (previously entitled 'Lead') was shortlisted for the Plough Prize 2009

'Bunker' was shortlisted for the Fish Poetry Prize 2010

'First Litter' was shortlisted for the Bridport Prize 2010